MÓTÓ
FAVORITES

ISBN 0-634-05761-8

HAL•LEONARD®
CORPORATION
7777 W. BLUEMOUND RD. P.O. BOX 13819 MILWAUKEE, WI 53213

Visit Hal Leonard Online at
www.halleonard.com

◆ ABC

CLARINET

Words and Music by
ALPHONSO MIZELL, FREDERICK PERREN,
DEKE RICHARDS and BERRY GORDY

② HEATWAVE
(Love Is Like A Heatwave)

CLARINET

Words and Music by EDWARD HOLLAND,
LAMONT DOZIER and BRIAN HOLLAND

❸ HOW SWEET IT IS
(To Be Loved By You)

CLARINET

Words and Music by EDWARD HOLLAND,
LAMONT DOZIER and BRIAN HOLLAND

◆ I HEARD IT THROUGH THE GRAPEVINE

8

CLARINET

Words and Music by
NORMAN J. WHITFIELD and BARRETT STRONG

◆⑤ MY GIRL

CLARINET

Words and Music by
WILLIAM "SMOKEY" ROBINSON and RONALD WHITE

◆ SHOP AROUND

CLARINET

Words and Music by
BERRY GORDY and WILLIAM "SMOKEY" ROBINSON

STOP! IN THE NAME OF LOVE

Clarinet

Words and Music by LAMONT DOZIER,
BRIAN HOLLAND and EDWARD HOLLAND

◆⑧ I CAN'T HELP MYSELF
(Sugar Pie, Honey Bunch)

CLARINET

Words and Music by BRIAN HOLLAND,
LAMONT DOZIER and EDWARD HOLLAND

Sax Solo

◆9 PLEASE MR. POSTMAN

CLARINET

Words and Music by ROBERT BATEMAN,
GEORGIA DOBBINS, WILLIAM GARRETT,
FREDDIE GORMAN and BRIAN HOLLAND

⬥ 10 YOU CAN'T HURRY LOVE

CLARINET

Words and Music by EDWARD HOLLAND,
LAMONT DOZIER and BRIAN HOLLAND

17

UPTIGHT
(Everything's Alright)

CLARINET

Words and Music by STEVIE WONDER,
SYLVIA MOY and HENRY COSBY

Moderately Fast

PLAY ALONG CD COLLECTIONS

BAND JAM

12 band favorites complete with accompaniment CD, including: Born to Be Wild • Danger Zone • Devil with the Blue Dress • Final Countdown • Get Ready for This • Gonna Make You Sweat (Everybody Dance Now) • I Got You (I Feel Good) • Rock & Roll - Part II (The Hey Song) • Twist and Shout • We Will Rock You • Wild Thing • Y.M.C.A.

_____	00841232 Flute	$10.95
_____	00841233 Clarinet	$10.95
_____	00841234 Alto Sax	$10.95
_____	00841235 Trumpet	$10.95
_____	00841236 Horn	$10.95
_____	00841237 Trombone	$10.95
_____	00841238 Violin	$10.95

DISNEY SOLOS – INTERMEDIATE LEVEL

An exciting collection of 12 solos with professional orchestral accompaniment on CD. Titles include: Be Our Guest • Can You Feel the Love Tonight • Colors of the Wind • Friend like Me • Under the Sea • You've Got a Friend in Me • Zero to Hero • and more.

_____	00841404 Flute	$12.95
_____	00841506 Oboe	$12.95
_____	00841405 Clarinet/Tenor Sax	$12.95
_____	00841406 Alto Sax	$12.95
_____	00841407 Horn	$12.95
_____	00841408 Trombone	$12.95
_____	00841409 Trumpet	$12.95
_____	00841410 Violin	$12.95
_____	00841411 Viola	$12.95
_____	00841412 Cello	$12.95
_____	00841553 Mallet Percussion	$12.95

EASY DISNEY FAVORITES

A fantastic selection of 13 Disney favorites for solo instuments, including: Bibbidi-Bobbidi-Boo • Candle on the Water • Chim Chim Cher-ee • A Dream Is a Wish Your Heart Makes • It's a Small World • Let's Go Fly a Kite • Mickey Mouse March • A Spoonful of Sugar • Supercalifragilisticexpialidocious • Toyland March • Winnie the Pooh • The Work Song • Zip-A-Dee-Doo-Dah. Each book features a play-along CD with complete rhythm section accompaniment.

_____	00841371 Flute	$10.95
_____	00841477 Clarinet	$10.95
_____	00841478 Alto Sax	$10.95
_____	00841479 Trumpet	$10.95
_____	00841480 Trombone	$10.95
_____	00841372 Violin	$10.95
_____	00841481 Viola	$10.95
_____	00841482 Cello/Bass	$10.95

FAVORITE MOVIE THEMES

13 themes, including: An American Symphony from *Mr. Holland's Opus* • Braveheart • Chariots of Fire • Forrest Gump – Main Title • Theme from *Jurassic Park* • Mission: Impossible Theme • and more.

_____	00841166 Flute	$10.95
_____	00841167 Clarinet	$10.95
_____	00841169 Alto Sax	$10.95
_____	00841168 Trumpet/Tenor Sax	$10.95
_____	00841171 Horn	$10.95
_____	00841170 Trombone	$10.95
_____	00841296 Violin	$10.95

HYMNS FOR THE MASTER

15 inspirational favorites, including: All Hail the Power of Jesus' Name • Amazing Grace • Crown Him With Many Crowns • Joyful, Joyful We Adore Thee • This Is My Father's World • When I Survey the Wondrous Cross • and more.

_____	00841136 Flute	$12.95
_____	00841137 Clarinet	$12.95
_____	00841138 Alto Sax	$12.95
_____	00841139 Trumpet	$12.95
_____	00841140 Trombone	$12.95
_____	00841239 Piano Accompaniment (no CD)	$8.95

JAZZ & BLUES

14 songs for solo instruments, complete with a play-along CD. Includes: Bernie's Tune • Cry Me a River • Fever • Fly Me to the Moon • God Bless' the Child • Harlem Nocturne • Moonglow • A Night in Tunisia • One Note Samba • Opus One • Satin Doll • Slightly Out of Tune (Desafinado) • Take the "A" Train • Yardbird Suite.

00841438 Flute	$10.95
00841439 Clarinet	$10.95
00841440 Alto Sax	$10.95
00841441 Trumpet	$10.95
00841442 Tenor Sax	$10.95
00841443 Trombone	$10.95
00841444 Violin	$10.95

MAMBO NO. 5, MARIA MARIA, AND OTHER LATIN HITS

These long-awaited play-along book/CD packs feature 10 super hot Latin hits: Genie in a Bottle • I Need to Know • I Wan'na Be like You (The Monkey Song) • If You Had My Love • Mambo No. 5 (A Little Bit Of...) • Mambo Swing • Maria Maria • Mucho Mambo • Para De Jugar • You Sang to Me.

00841526 Flute	$10.95
00841527 Clarinet	$10.95
00841528 Alto Sax	$10.95
00841529 Tenor Sax	$10.95
00841530 Trumpet	$10.95
00841531 Horn	$10.95
00841532 Trombone	$10.95
00841533 Violin	$10.95

PLAY THE DUKE

Features 11 classics from Duke Ellington's stellar career: Caravan • Don't Get Around Much Anymore • I Got It Bad and That Ain't Good • I'm Beginning to See the Light • In a Sentimental Mood • It Don't Mean a Thing (If It Ain't Got That Swing) • Mood Indigo • Satin Doll • Solitude • Sophisticated Lady • Take the "A" Train.

00841515 Flute	$10.95
00841516 Clarinet	$10.95
00841517 Alto Sax	$10.95
00841518 Tenor Sax	$10.95
00841519 Trumpet	$10.95
00841520 Horn	$10.95
00841521 Trombone	$10.95
00841522 Violin	$10.95

ROCK JAMS

12 rockin' favorites to jam along with the accompanying CD. Songs include: Addicted to Love • Another One Bites the Dust • Get Ready • Love Shack • What I Like About You • and more.

_____	00841251 Flute	$10.95
_____	00841252 Clarinet/Tenor Sax	$10.95
_____	00841253 Alto Sax	$10.95
_____	00841254 Trumpet	$10.95
_____	00841257 Horn	$10.95
_____	00841255 Trombone/Baritone	$10.95
_____	00841256 Violin	$10.95

Prices, contents, and availability subject to change without notice.

FROM

FOR MORE INFORMATION, SEE YOUR LOCAL MUSIC DEALER, OR WRITE TO:

HAL•LEONARD® CORPORATION

7777 W. BLUEMOUND RD. P.O. BOX 13819 MILWAUKEE, WI 53213

http://www.halleonard.com